ENGLAND, ARISE!

MICK MARTIN
ENGLAND, ARISE!

Francis
Boutle
Publishers

First published by Francis Boutle Publishers
272 Alexandra Park Road
London N22 7BG
020 8889 7744
www.francisboutle.co.uk

ISBN 978 1 903427 96 5

Acknowledgements

Special thanks first and foremost to Cyril Pearce, without whom we would have no knowledge of this story. His work in *Comrades in Conscience* has enabled us to create the play and his tireless support and encouragement and advice at every stage of the project has been invaluable. Similarly Jill Liddington's book, *Rebel Girls*, has played a major part in our process and introduced us to women like Lavena Saltonstall and Lilian Lenton who we were so inspired by. Thanks to Ralph Dartford and Tanya Geier Thomson at Arts Council England steadfastly championed the project for us at every turn, and all at the Amiel & Melburn Trust, the Lipman-Miliband Trust and Co-op Community Foundation their generous support for the project; Kim Strickson and Pauline Lawton at Kirklees Community Heritage Team for being so supportive and also including us as part of their centenary project; Victoria Firth and all at Lawrence Batley Theatre for all their support; Jen Sullivan at Dep Arts who worked to book the tour for us; Barney for bringing his keen eye and mind to the project; Nez for making such a fine promo video of the R&D week; Jamie and Lee for their musical inputs and all round cheery disposition; Ruth Potts and Molly Conisbee for their radical pamphleteering and walks; Dr Janette Martin and Dr Rebecca Gill of Huddersfield University History Department for all their support and advice too; and Hannah Batley and Siobhan Donnelly, our erstwhile student placements. Lastly, as ever, the actors who came on board at the start of the R&D project and became part of our whole group, for all their commitment, enthusiasm and skill in bringing the project to life. We are extremely grateful for all the help and encouragement we have received on this project and sincerely hope that we have done it and all involved justice.

Preface

In the 1960s, public life in this country was still enriched by the presence of men and women who had been alive and politically active during the First World War. Many of them still held office of some kind, others were on the verge of retirement. It was then, as a post-graduate student, that I had the privilege of meeting a number of the Huddersfield men and women who had played active parts in the Labour and Socialist movement since before 1914. Among them was the central character in this play, Arthur Gardiner. Sadly I was never able to talk to his best friend, Percy Ellis, but Arthur and fellow Socialist, Wilfrid Whiteley, and, much later, the wonderful Florence Shaw, told me a story of Huddersfield's history which neither I nor, it seems, anyone else at the time, had heard before. It was a story which boldly asserted that during the First World War Huddersfield had been 'special'. First, because of the number of its young men who refused military service as conscientious objectors, and second, because of the extent to which their stand against the war was tolerated and even supported across the community. It is that story that I tried to understand in writing my book *Comrades in Conscience*.

Setting aside any notion that here was special pleading on behalf of their home town and their political views, my research discovered that Huddersfield had, indeed, been 'special' during the war in the extent and vigour of its war-resister community of which Arthur Gardiner was one of its charismatic figures. But this was not simply a matter of individual conscience. Huddersfield's conscientious objectors came from and were supported by a community which drew on the town's pre-war radical politics. In doing so it included significant contributions from the women's movement, suffragists as well as suffragettes, Socialists of all kinds, trade unionists and members of many of the town's religious groups, especially the Quakers.

Looking back on that time, now a hundred years ago, it is difficult to get a proper sense of what it was like to take a stand against the war. Wartime censorship under the Defence of the Realm Act, press self-censorship and the post-war destruction of many key documents, have helped erect a barrier of smoke and mirrors between now and then. Nevertheless, it is very clear that it was hard to be a conscientious objector. Press hostility, savage government propaganda, prison sentences and army brutality have not been under-estimated. Arthur's experiences as a conscientious objector have something to say about all these things. But it is also true that Arthur's story, and that of his friend Percy Ellis and those of the hundred other Huddersfield conscientious objectors, are not just their stories but parts of the story of a particular community at a particular time which chose to stand against the war and all that it meant.

But, was Huddersfield the only place in Britain during the First World War that was 'special' in this way? When *Comrades in Conscience* was first published in 2001 the absence of other research suggested that it might have been. However, since then, further work on war resisters, taking in the whole of England, Scotland and Wales, has begun to suggest a different view. It is now clear that there were a great many other 'Huddersfields' and in many different parts of the country. It is also clear that although Arthur was a hero to Huddersfield's war resister community, there were a great many other 'Arthurs' who were just as important in their own home towns.

The Imperial War Museum has now adopted the database which has made these new insights possible. In the autumn of 2014, the *Pearce Register of British First World War Conscientious Objectors* will go on line as part of the Imperial War Museum's Lives of the First World War website. Access to all users will be completely free and their additions and corrections will be received, reviewed and added. New and revised versions based on on-going research will be published at regular intervals. With the database as a guide it will now be possible for people to trace their own CO ancestors and for others to explore the real stories of war resisters across the country. Perhaps, by the end of the of the First World War centenary commemoration period, we will then be able to write a new history of the people's feelings about the war and give the war resisters their proper place.

December 2013's public reading of the first draft of the script of *England, Arise!* at Huddersfield's Lawrence Batley Theatre brought all these issues home. Working with Mick Martin, Jude Wright and the team of young actors they had recruited for the show was the kind of experience that historians don't often get. Research and writing take you to one level of understanding but having to re-visit the material to help create characters, settings and moments which can be given a theatrical reality is much more challenging. Seeing and hearing academic research brought to the stage gave it an immediacy which even the best writing has difficulty in achieving. The audience response was quite remarkable – enthusiastic, positive and questioning. Many were asking 'Why hasn't this story been told before?'. They clearly wanted more and this new edition of the play is a powerful response to that need.

Cyril Pearce
August 2014

Foreword

Every now and again a story stands up and hits you in the face with its combination of truth, power and humanity, its drama. The largely unknown story of Arthur Gardiner, a dyers labourer from Huddersfield, who refused to fight in the First World War on account of his political beliefs, is such a one. This play is inspired by and built around the verbatim account of Arthur's bravura performance before the Military Service Tribunal in 1916, when they tried and failed to catch out this cocksure, confident and utterly engaging young mill labourer. It was he who ran rings around them.

100 years later Arthur's story speaks to us on numerous levels, and the similarities with our own time are abundant. On the one hand we have a good old-fashioned David and Goliath tale of the little guy from Huddersfield who the Establishment could not beat. But the closer we looked at it, the more we saw a much broader and more nuanced narrative, one that takes us beyond the traditional image of working-class northerners. These radical Socialist COs were not operating in isolation, they were linked to and part of a much wider consciousness, that crossed class boundaries, that was seeking to change, to revolutionize the world around it in a whole host of different ways.

Foremost in this must be the women's suffrage movement. There was an amazing array of northern women from all backgrounds, campaigning tirelessly. Jill Liddington in her book *Rebel Girls* provides an invaluable insight into the world of these women, many of whom would otherwise be forgotten now. Arthur and his good friend Percy Ellis were not just supported by the women, but also inspired by them. By 1914 women had been imprisoned and gone on hunger strike, the cat and mouse act had seen them being chased and harassed as fugitives, prepared to create havoc, and risk their own lives for the principle they believed in. The benchmark was set, the challenge was thrown down. But were the men up to it?

At the same time as this, the revolutionary movements in the world of Art and Literature, Cubism, Post-Impressionism, the Futurists et al, serve to underline the sense that fundamental change was on the way. A new and deeper way of seeing, understanding the world around was taking root. Revolution was in the air, the old order was no longer sustainable at the start of a new century, one of mechanized industry and technological advances seemingly unthinkable only a few years before, a new dawn was on the horizon.

It is in this world, where these young men and women believe change is not just possible but inevitable, that Arthur and Percy confronted the Military Tribunals and made their stance against conscription and militarism. They did so with such conviction because they knew they were not alone.

A picture of our forebears 100 years ago began to emerge that contradicts the received wisdom of mass support for the war. Arthur and Percy were part of a much wider protest movement than conventional history tells us. The story of the anti-war movement has been airbrushed out of the narrative, it is one we are more than happy to play our part in placing it back with the prominence it deserves.

We have sought to capture the passion and intensity of these young people, the real urgency of the moment, of the revolutionary times they lived in, but also a sense of their hope, humour and optimism for a better tomorrow, in spite of everything. They wanted to change the world and believed that they could. When you compare that to our own times, when young people are supposed to be cynical, and turned off politics, that is an important message.

Dramatizing their story has been a great challenge, but also a real privilege. We are indebted to Cyril Pearce for his book *Comrades in Conscience*, without which we would not have been able to mount this production. In the course of it we have had to make choices about which characters to include and which to leave out and it's been unfair on some, such as Edith Key and Fred Shaw, but we hope that our play serves as an introduction to this story and fascinating piece of history and that after seeing or reading it, people will be inspired to read on and discover more for themselves.

Mick Martin & Jude Wright
September, 2014
www.bentarchitect.co.uk

A note on the play

This is an ensemble piece, so any lines of text not specifically assigned to a character form part of the overall narrative device, i.e., that of the Clarion Socialist Dramatic Society performing the play, and so can be given to whichever cast member is most convenient at the time.

There are a selection of the Socialist Hymns printed at the end of the script; these were the ones we used in the play. 'England, Arise!' obviously selects itself, but the others can be used at the director/ musical director's discretion. They were not performed in full, but used in small pieces during the course of the action, perhaps one verse, and used as codas, interludes between scenes or as underscoring. Music was played live by the actors.

ENGLAND, ARISE!

CAST LIST

Arthur Gardiner	Chris Lindon
Percy Ellis	James Britton
Sis Timmins	Laura Bonnah
Lavena Saltonstall/	
Lilian Lenton/various	Stephanie Butler
Isaac Timmins/Alfred Orage/	
John Hunter Watts/various	Matthew Booth
Director	Jude Wright
Designer	Barney George
Musical Directors	Jamie Lockhart & Lee Smith
Historical Advisor	Cyril Pearce
Producers	Bent Architect
Poster design and artwork	Tricia McGrath

First performed at The Lawrence Batley Theatre, Huddersfield, on 24 October 2014.

SCENE 1 / INTRO

The stage is set a la The Huddersfield Socialist Sunday School, 1914. On the wall are the Socialist Ten Commandments.

The cast (and audience) sing the Socialist anthem – England Arise! *–*

We are the Clarion Socialist Dramatic Society. Tonight, for you, we will perform our play ... *England, Arise!*

We begin in Huddersfield. A place of Liberals, non-Conformists, Socialists and soapboxes, suffragettes and suffragists.

It is early summer 1914.

We're in the Socialist Sunday School, with Arthur Gardiner, a dyers' labourer at Zetland Mills.

Arthur has a pen and paper in hand, working out a speech.

ARTHUR: Comrades!

And his mate, Percy Ellis, a book-keeper.

PERCY: Afternoon all. First job, kettle on...

ARTHUR: The revolution shall not be achieved...

PERCY: Without a proper brew of tea.

ARTHUR: And a full dissection of the football results.

PERCY: Will Town get promoted?

ARTHUR: The short answer? No.

PERCY: The long answer?

ARTHUR: Never.

PERCY: Day like this, sun cracking the flags, we should be out playing football, cricket, rugby league even.

ARTHUR: I played yesterday.

PERCY: Did you win?

ARTHUR: Let's just say the ref had Liberal tendencies. Straight as a dye to your face and a two-faced chiseller behind your back!

PERCY: You always say that! What score were it?

1

ARTHUR: (*sheepish*) That's not the point. (*pause*) 48 ... two

PERCY: 48–two!?

ARTHUR: I scored the two mind! Now, comrades, ask yourselves this...

PERCY: Where's the milk?

ARTHUR: What?

PERCY: For the tea.

Enter LAVENA, *with some milk.*

LAVENA: Afternoon boys.

Lavena Saltonstall, a tailoress from Hebden Bridge.

LAVENA: I know.

I'm telling them, they don't, do they?

LAVENA: I'm with you.

PERCY: Eh up, Lavena, Clarion Cycling Club trip next Saturday, Peak District, you coming?

LAVENA: I'd love to Percy but some toilet-mouthed little chuff in Todmorden busted Boadicea last week.

ARTHUR: Busted who?

LAVENA: Boadicea! my faithful, trusty chariotess, my bicycle!

PERCY: Outrageous!

LAVENA: His beery dad, stood with a grin like Gordale Scar!

Get home and mend your husband's socks! No wonder you're all bloody spinsters! If you were my wife I'd feed you poison!

LAVENA: No sir you would not...

Why not?

LAVENA: Cos I'd have already fed it to you!

ARTHUR: Good line.

LAVENA: And danced on your grave.

Bit severe.

LAVENA: Naked!

Go easy.

LAVENA: Yes I am unmarried – this is what I said back to him...

PERCY: Got you, carry on.

LAVENA: Yes, I am unmarried and strange as it may seem to you I have no intention to marry either, because living in an age when vice and disease are stalking the land and attacking the people of my class ... I have decided to abandon the so called womanly accomplishments and have something to say about these evils!

PERCY: What happened then?

LAVENA: Loads of 'em cheered! One woman wept, another called me a lesbodlian.

ARTHUR: A what?

LAVENA: Aye. A feller called Norris asked if I'd go out with him and cried when I said no, then all the little scufflers spat at us, threw eggs, cauliflower, spuds.

PERCY: Could have lobbed a lump of bacon in.

ARTHUR: You'd have your dinner.

LAVENA: Todmorden, strange place.

PERCY: Neither Yorkshire nor Lancashire.

ARTHUR: Dark nor light. Wet nor dry.

PERCY: It is curious ... indeterminate.

ARTHUR: And hilly as a fat lad's gut.

LAVENA: So I was going to ask if School funds could pay for Boadicea's resurrection? Needs a new chain and a front wheel.

PERCY: Ah. We're flat broke.

ARTHUR: Course we can, we need you and Boadicea out there, Lavena, covering the ground!

PERCY: Er, you asked me to look at the Sunday School books. We're bust.

ARTHUR: Stop thinking like they do ... money, money, money ... we need to fire up the masses with *ideas*!

PERCY: Arthur I'm a book-keeper. I don't have ideas! Stuff either adds up or it doesn't. Our outgoings exceed income ... projected loss for the year 1914 is £12.10s.

ARTHUR: Giddy me! £12.10s? That's the revolution down the swanney and out to sea isn't it? We can't put off by things like that.

PERCY: No but we can be put out of these premises. Just saying.

LAVENA: We need more members.

ARTHUR: And we'll get 'em. Just look at the classes we're offering this year! For starters, Introduction to Marxism. We also offer Elementary Marxism ... then there's Intermediate Marxism ... and the ever-popular Advanced Marxism.

PERCY: And for the kids?

ARTHUR: For the 12 to 14 year olds, What Marxism Means Today.

LAVENA: And for the four to seven year olds?

PERCY: What Marxism means Tomorrow? Followed by basic toilet skills?

ARTHUR: Bless their little hearts, happy carefree days, eh.

LAVENA: Blimey Arthur, we need a more personal touch ... reach out to people on things that matter to them ... make 'em think ... ask questions, like...

Enter SIS, *holding a leaflet.*

SIS: Is this where the Drama Group meets?

PERCY: Eh?

LAVENA: Is this where the ... what?

ARTHUR: No it's where the Socialist Sunday School meet.

SIS: Can't be a right good one.

LAVENA: And why not?

SIS: Or he'd know to say pardon and not 'eh'!

PERCY: Eh?

Oh, sorry, missed my cue, ladies and gentlemen, Sis Timmins.

Sis: I know.

They don't do they? Bit of patience might not go amiss, Miss.

Sis: Yes alright, do you mind? I saw a poster in the Co-op butcher's window for the Clarion Drama Group.

Percy: You're in the right place.

Lavena: At the wrong time.

Story of my life.

Arthur: Monday is Clarion Drama Group.

Percy: Tuesday is Clarion Cycling Club

Lavena: Wednesday is Clarion Athletics Club

Arthur: Thursday is Clarion Choir practice.

Lavena: Friday is Clarion Traditional Dancing.

Arthur: Or basket weaving for those of a less energetic disposition.

Percy: Saturday is Clarion Beer club!

Lavena: There is no Clarion beer club. Too many men spending all the wage in the pub and none left for the housekeeping … we need to make 'em think, ask questions like – Missis, do you want something better for your daughters than what you had yourself? In my native place the women wash every Monday, iron Tuesdays, court on Wednesday, bake on Thursdays, clean on Fridays, go to market or go courting again on Saturdays, and to church on Sundays.

Sis: As long as they've done the washing and ironing and been to church I see no harm in a spot of courting.

Lavena: There are exceptions of course, hundreds, but they are considered unwomanly, eccentric people. If girls develop any craving for a different life or wider ideas, their mothers fear they are going to become Socialists … or Suffragettes! A Socialist being a person with lax views about other people's watches and purses. And a suffragette…

Sis: A person whose house is always untidy.

Lavena: I think you'll find suffragettes very different from the things you've been told Miss…?

SIS: Timmins … Miss…?

LAVENA: Saltonstall. It's rough, dangerous at times, a lot of walking … but it's also a lot of fun. My favourite was when Winston Churchill came to the Free Trade Hall in Manchester. We took turns during his speech to leap up and shout Votes For Women!

SIS: What happened?

LAVENA: We all got arrested. But we made 'em listen. Same as when we marched on London … thousands of us … banners streaming, colours everywhere … what a day!

SIS: What happened?

LAVENA: We all got arrested!

SIS: Right. That's not so different from what I've heard, actually.

LAVENA: I was accused of assaulting a police officer. The judge asked 'well young Miss…' just like that, really patronising … 'young Miss … what have you to say for yourself?' … I replied – I have nothing to say except he resisted me in the execution on my duty.

SIS: Were you not afraid? In London?

LAVENA: No … best thing I've ever done. A revolution in itself. No home life, no one to say what we should do or not do, no family ties. We were free and alone in a great city. Scores of young women scarcely out of their teens. You've no idea what it felt like.

SIS: I'd never dare do anything like that.

LAVENA: That's what I thought. And why it was so incredible! Now, since you're here, cast an eye over these plays, we need to choose our autumn production soon.

LAVENA *gives* SIS *a selection of plays.* ARTHUR *takes* PERCY *aside.*

ARTHUR: Who's she? Newcomer?

PERCY: Sis Timmins. She's a mender. Her old feller's Isaac Timmins.

ARTHUR: Oh. Isaac Timmins, builder?

PERCY: And staunch Liberal.

ARTHUR: *Liberal*!? Imagine bringing up a rare flower like that.

PERCY: An orchid.

ARTHUR: In an ideological compost heap.

PERCY: A turnip patch!

ARTHUR: Like *Liberalism*!

PERCY: Shameful.

ARTHUR: Heartbreaking.

PERCY: Cruel.

ARTHUR: Nay, immoral. Percy, I cannot stand by and see the poor thing suffer in ignorance.

PERCY: I understand brother. Your intentions are purely Marxist.

ARTHUR *turns his attentions to* SIS.

LAVENA: Right, our autumn drama production, proposals are as follow…

SIS: 'Major Barbara' by George Bernard Shaw.

LAVENA: Or an adaptation of Victor Hugo's 'Les Miserables' called 'The Bishop's Candlesticks'.

SIS: Oh I don't fancy 'Les Miserables'.

LAVENA: Why not?

SIS: It's miserable. I might like it if there were *songs* in it.

ARTHUR: Sacrilege!

LAVENA: Brilliant idea!

PERCY: Defile a Socialist text with *songs*?!

LAVENA: It's an adaptation of part of 'Les Miserables', so it might be the happier bits.

SIS: Won't be right long then.

LAVENA: 'Major Barbara'? Or 'Les Miserables'?

PERCY: I quite fancy 'The Bishop's Candlestick'.

ARTHUR: Yes I've heard it's very powerful.

PERCY: It's not short either.

LAVENA: I say Major Barbara.

SIS: Agreed

ARTHUR: Well that's two for 'The Bishop's CandleStick' and two for 'Major Barbara'.

PERCY: (*pause*) So ... er, Major Barbara it is then.

LAVENA: Percy you're getting it, there's hope for you yet.

LAVENA/SIS: I shall take the part of Major Bar ... bara...

LAVENA: Oh. Unless you want to, Sis?

SIS: Oh no, no, Lavena you must, you'd be very good I don't doubt.

LAVENA: No it's you, I can see it now, it's you.

SIS: Agreed! I'll be quite wonderful.

LAVENA: Rehearsals start next week. Right I've to be off, campaigning in Mirfield at six! Don't weaken boys, it's only eggs and fruit!

Scene 2

ARTHUR *and* SIS *remain alone.*

SIS: I've seen you before.

ARTHUR: When's that, then?

SIS: St George's Square. I like to go of a Saturday when you're all on your soapboxes shouting. It's like the fairground.

ARTHUR: First place I ever heard the word ... Socialism. I was walking up Northumberland St, big crowd in't Square, I thought, eh up, is there a fight going off? But it was a Socialist meeting.

SIS: Is it not the same thing?

ARTHUR: Not at the start, by the end I grant you. I listened, even bought a pamphlet. I read it. It was like some kind gadger understood me at last, had thrown this lost soul a copper to put in my heart's gas meter, and fire up the lights in my head. I was converted to the path of revolution!

SIS: Do you write poetry?

ARTHUR: No.

8

SIS: Don't start. You sound just like some when they first get chapel. Arthur, people don't want a revolution.

ARTHUR: How do you know? We just need the right conditions, strikes, social turmoil, food shortages, riots.

SIS: Oh, smashing. People want *money*. A piano, even if they can't play it, hand-made curtains the neighbours can't afford, to send sweet Cecilia to ballet and elocution classes! To be that little bit *better*. You can't change that.

ARTHUR: I want them to be better as well. Folk'll see it, Sis ... stands to reason. But we'll have to tear down the entire system and chase off all their priests and vicars to do it.

SIS: You'll burn in the fires of hell, Arthur Gardiner!

ARTHUR: Come with me.

SIS: To hell?

ARTHUR: No, Leeds, on Friday, to a talk at the Mechanics Institute? A feller called Alfred Orage. I'll buy you a port and lemon after.

SIS: I don't drink alcohol.

ARTHUR: Just lemon then.

SIS: Alfred Orange?

ARTHUR: Orage. He's part of Leeds Arts Club.

SIS: What's that?

ARTHUR: It's an Arts Club.

SIS: In Leeds?

ARTHUR: Aye. It's a place for ideas. Ideas they don't want us having. We're getting six o'clock train on Friday.

SIS: I'll think about it. I have to go now.

ARTHUR: Till Friday.

SIS: You don't know if I'll come.

ARTHUR: I live in hope ... eat, sleep and breathe it, it's all I have, Sis Timmins, owner of the most kissable cheek in all the West Riding.

SCENE 3

Enter ISAAC TIMMINS, *50, large. He takes a seat, as if awaiting his dinner.* SIS *waits on him, taking his boots off etc. Then she brings him his dinner on a tray.*

Ladies and gentlemen, boys and girls, Mr Isaac Timmins returns from his labours, to his sturdy Yorkshire terrace, parlour front and back and its own private privy!

ISAAC: Least a feller deserves. Peace for a private shi...

It lies just up the hill from the perfumed little town, and its sweet scented canals.

ISAAC: Bloody stinks down there!

It in't so good in that privy when you've been in.

ISAAC: Brass off.

SIS: Father, language! We're in the front parlour! We haven't paid a fortune for these curtains for you to swear at them.

ISAAC: My bloody front parlour isn't it? Now, who's the lippy chippy little bottle-smashing Bolshevik you were dallying with yesterday then?

SIS: I'm sure I've no idea, and even if I was it wouldn't be anybody else's business.

ISAAC: You're my daughter and it's my business. I see him up in St George's Square, spreading revolution like the blasted smallpox.

SIS: You seem to know a lot about him, more than I do that's for sure

ISAAC: He's the sort you notice.

SIS: Arthur Gardiner?

ISAAC: Aha! So you do know him then? Oho ho, you can't fool the old man!

SIS: I may know him. He's right enough, but you wouldn't look at him twice.

ISAAC: Him and his mate. That Percy. Another flaming rebel, going through town t'other week with a donkey, I don't know who were leading who, them or the ass!

SIS: I have no idea what you're talking about.

10

ISAAC: I have no time for tuppeny rabble rousers, Socialists, Suffragists, Bradford City supporters. What the hell's going on today?

SIS: Who's to say any of 'em like you?

ISAAC: I don't want you consorting with *Arthur Gardiner*. I don't like him or his sort. I wouldn't care, but a thrumpin' dyehouse labourer's all he is.

SIS: What's it matter what he is?

ISAAC: It matters to me. He lives down Millford St for God's sake, rough as a badgers arse!

SIS: Don't curse in the front parlour! After all we're so much better than folk in Milford St aren't wc?

ISAAC: Yes we bloo ... we are. Filch the grub out of your gullet they would! Steal the smoke out of your pipe, the butter off the bread, the...

SIS: Yes alright.

ISAAC: Between Socialists and the flamin Irish ... Home rule! The cheek. It's in the paper this morning, stealing guns, shooting at policemen.

SIS: I don't think Arthur steals guns and shoots policemen ... (*then wonders*) least I don't think he does. Then again, now you say it...

ISAAC: You don't know what they'd do ... give 'em a chance. Socialists, Irish...

SIS: Irish Socialists.

ISAAC: Ye gods, what a thought! Sis ... I only want what's best for you.

SIS: They pull quite a crowd in't Square. Arthur gets very passionate up on his soapbox. God knows what he's on about but...

ISAAC: Never mind what he's on about! My final word. Now I'll go to the Liberal Club, glass of ale, serious conversation. Isaac Timmins has spoken.

Exit ISAAC.

SIS: And Sis Timmins has listened. Too many times.

SCENE 4

ARTHUR *and* PERCY *wait for* SIS.

Friday evening St George's Square ... lo! the clock approaches six.

PERCY: She'll not come.

ARTHUR: She'll come.

PERCY: She'll not come. Old iron drawers Timmins let his prize petal out with the likes of us? Never!

ARTHUR: Happen you're right. He'll be in't Liberal Club right now won't he?

ARTHUR *and* PERCY *do their impressions of* ISAAC *as* LAVENA *enters.*

ARTHUR: A glass of ale with fellow men of business!

PERCY: The cigar smoking classes.

ARTHUR: Property owning folks.

PERCY: The bed rock of the district!

ARTHUR: See this arse!

PERCY: It's made of solid Yorkshire stone!

ARTHUR: Boot it and you'd break your blinkin' foot lad!

PERCY: Well you won't have to worry cos she's not coming.

ARTHUR: She'll come ... I hope. Hope is all we have Percy.

PERCY: Come on how many times have you been stood up?

LAVENA: Arthur sweetheart there's folk think you're a statue you're stood here that often.

PERCY: I've had to wipe bird muck off him before now.

Sudden sharp cut away to SIS, *across stage, alone.*

SIS: (*nervous*) Father ... I'm ... I'm going to a ... to a young ladies ... erm ... social evening at chapel ... so ... don't wait up ... I have to go, bye!

She is out, and runs like hell on the spot, looking over her shoulder as she goes.

PERCY: We're gonna miss train ... she's not coming ... face it you've been stood up. Again.

SIS *running full tilt, she stops, gathers herself, saunters jauntily over to them all.*

ARTHUR: Aha! What did I tell you!

LAVENA: Faith and patience is rewarded!

ARTHUR: Remember that Percy.

SIS: Evening. Now, what's this about the two of you in town with a donkey?

ARTHUR: The Daily Herald wrote some codswallop about us.

PERCY: So as a lighthearted riposte to this editorial bias.

PERCY: We released a fellow worker from his bondage at the fairground.

ARTHUR: Welcomed our hairy-faced cousin into our Socialist family.

SIS: You stole a donkey?

ARTHUR: We took him back afterwards.

PERCY: We hung a sign on him that said:

ARTHUR: "*I'd sooner be an ass than read the Daily Herald*" and went up through town with it.

PERCY: It made people laugh. Well it made us laugh. Mind we'd had a few.

SCENE 5

A flourishing musical introduction. Enter ALFRED ORAGE. *He is extravagantly dressed. All are taken in by his powerful and charismatic presence.*

ORAGE: I, am Orage!

Mr Alfred Orage – founder of the Leeds Arts Club...

ORAGE: I know.

I'm telling them! And one time Socialist, currently editor of the New Age magazine, in that London.

The cast do a collective oooh at the mention of London.

LAVENA: London. Cheeky chappies.

SIS: And ridiculously overpriced beverages and other comestibles.

13

ORAGE *clears his throat, sets himself and begins. He speaks with fluid passion, yet is light and dexterous in his delivery. As he speaks the cast shout and cheer in agreement as if he were a live band.*

ORAGE: Orage will begin. The subject this evening is Art and Revolution.

Art and politics in this modern industrialized age are not to be kept in discreet boxes. The energy of cubism, I think of the genius of Matisse, Braque, of Pablo Picasso here, and the growing world of literature and music they inspire, Schoenberg is one example ... are definitive signs of the times and should be read, and seen, as profoundly, political ... and truly ... *revolutionary!*

LAVENA: Yes indeed!

ORAGE: Cubism. The relationship of the viewer to the painting, the conventional means of seeing is *broken* ... dislocated ... the image is made strange, reassembled ... to be seen anew. To be seen ... *truly!* We are no longer slaves to one singular vantage point, one *autocratic* way of perceiving, understanding, handed down from on high as it were. In this sense these artists challenge the established order of everything!

ARTHUR: What do you think Sis?

SIS: I think it's smashing!

ORAGE: The Leeds Arts Club are presently exhibiting work by Kandinsky, Gauguin, Van Gogh, and Klee ... as well as the finest of the modern English painters.

LAVENA: They're incredible!

ORAGE: Post Impressionism, in its quest to reach, to see beyond the immediate, into truths that are present yet hidden, is a revelation! The visible manifestation of a deeper consciousness.

LAVENA: And it is this seeing...?

ORAGE: Beyond...?

SIS: The merely literal...

LAVENA: And immediate?

ORAGE: To the underlying truths.

ARTHUR: That will free us from the shackles?

14

PERCY: Of class?

LAVENA: Gender?

SIS: Role?

ORAGE: And other apparently ... pre-ordained ... orientations.

SIS: *(pause)* pre-ordained ... orientations ... Mr Orage I'm not sure I...?

ORAGE: Consider this, at your leisure. Now ... it is with *great* sadness ... that Orage must tell you the arts of painting and of music today, are like voices prophesying ... war!

LAVENA: Oh heavens.

ORAGE: Artists, the true ones ... are the real soothsayers and visionaries ... Orage sees only catastrophe in their visions. Stravinsky, Schoenberg ... heralds of something dark I am sure.

ARTHUR: Could be a good thing.

LAVENA: How could the kind of carnage which a modern war, fought with the mechanized armaments...

PERCY: That they're making millions out of.

SIS: Ever be a *good* thing?

ORAGE: The Napoleonic wars will seem as nothing but playing compared to the coming conflict.

ARTHUR: Because these are revolutionary times!

PERCY: Ordinary folk'll see through it. It stands to reason!

ORAGE: It is education and culture that will save the working class, and hence my own, from a nightmare of anarchy and revolution.

ARTHUR: But Mr Orage ... we don't want to save it from revolution.

ORAGE: And neither do I! But in a cultural, even ... *spiritual* sense ... but Socialism ... has lost its direction.

Shock horror! All up on their feet to remonstrate.

LAVENA: Hold your horses!

PERCY: Steady on!

ARTHUR: Up on the reins old pal!

15

SIS: Explain yourself man!

ORAGE: Hear me out! England is necessary to Socialism, as Socialism is necessary to the world...

Now all nod and agree, that's far more like it!

I remember when William Morris, at the dawn of the movement some 25 years since, painted for us a portrait of ... *Utopia*, in his beautiful book, News From Nowhere. A Socialism of such hope ... such beauty...

ARTHUR: I read it.

SIS: (*impressed*) I've never even heard of it.

ARTHUR: I'll lend it you.

SIS: Okay.

ORAGE: When men and women of every kind and class, from weavers and miners to poets and artists, clerks and shop men, gathered together to contemplate a true fellowship, something ... beautiful!

Now he builds himself into the role of William Morris.

Morris looked into our faces, but his penetrating eyes seemed to suggest far away thoughts...

One lost the sense of the grimy city with its jostling thousands living under a pall of smoke ... One lost the sense of those small worries and oft time ridiculous conventions which oppress the soul and make life ... a weariness. One saw a reconquest of the green and beautiful England by a happy and healthy people...

But that is back when Socialism ... was *inspiring* ... that it would entail not simply the abolition of private property, but also the senseless division between art, life, and work ... it breathed ... *hope*!

LAVENA: We have hope Mr Orage.

PERCY: We live on it.

ORAGE: Socialism in that era had not yet become the prisoner of a particular, party machine ... a machine that associates its own well-being and the prospects for socialism as one and the same thing.

ARTHUR: But how do we make it work *without* a party machine?

ORAGE: Orage would ask how can you make it work *with* a party machine? The revolution I wish to see is not simply of the physical world ... but in our very *essence*. These are the original ... driving forces behind the movement ... a vision of Utopia. We must unshackle the *mind*, release the *spirit* ... and celebrate the *body*.

SIS: Oh my goodness.

ORAGE: Art will liberate the souls, and the minds of all.

SIS: Yes!

LAVENA: Nothing that is beautiful will harm the workers! Mr Orage!

ORAGE: Speak.

LAVENA: I am a tailoress, people think it is my burden to make trousers and vests, to knit and crochet, to sew and thank God for my station in life.

ORAGE: But no...

PERCY: No!

SIS: Oh no!

LAVENA: They think I ought to concern myself over clean doorsteps and sideboard covers ... I am supposed to make myself generally *useless* by ignoring things that matter – literature,

SIS: Music!

ORAGE: Art.

LAVENA: History.

ARTHUR: Marxism!

PERCY: Economics! Socialism adds up Mr Orage – Capitalism does not!

LAVENA: Mr Orage I cannot tell you what it's like to be able to feel ... be treated as an equal ... discuss ideas and not just be a mute worker!

ORAGE: I fully agree! Our goal is the emancipation of the spirit, a Socialism of fellowship among one and all.

ALL: Yes! Oh yes! This is it!

ORAGE: Not of tawdry class antagonism...

17

ALL: No!

ARTHUR/PERCY: Well...

ORAGE: Not of war or destruction...

ALL: No no!!

ORAGE: But of love!

LAVENA: Love!

ORAGE: Ultimately of free love!

All stop dead at that.

SIS: Sorry ... Mr Orage? What is *free* love?

ORAGE: We hold marriage to be an instrument of state oppression ... that the union of adults is no business of church or state ... and should be at their own discretion, free of shame, or shackles of any form.

SIS: Heavens.

LAVENA: To Mytholmroyd.

PERCY: And back.

SIS: Via Harrogate.

PERCY: Bloody hell.

ORAGE: That men and women ought be the sole judges of their own ... *orientation* in this regard, and do so ... in any combination.

Pause. Orage allows this to sink in.

SIS: Any ... any ... in any ... com ... com ... bination, Mr Orage? Of ... man ... and woman ... or ... and ...?

ORAGE: Oh yes. These are revolutionary ideas and times ... in *every* sense. We are in the *modern* era now.

SIS: Giddy me, I wasn't when I left home.

ORAGE: Orage fears a Socialism that *narrows* the mind ... rather than *expands* it ... and expands it to the furthest conceivable degree. Consider this.

And so friends I say to you that the Arts of today are bound together

18

with Politics ... and it is the duty of each to free the individual ... for the glory of living.

Leeds you've been a wonderful audience, Orage will return next year with further wondrous ideas and insight! I thankyou and good night!

Exit Orage. They are cheering, clapping, whistling and stamping for an encore.

And so Alfred Orage, founder of the Leeds Arts Club, editor of New Age magazine, prophet, visionary and sadly neglected figure in our social and cultural history, departs our stage and may I say how well performed his role was.

SIS: He was amazing!

LAVENA: What a thing it is ... for people like us to be able to make our mark ... with art and poetry ... right, I'm away, up first thing, I'm walking to Saddleworth then campaigning all day up on't tops! I love it. Night night!

ALL: Night night, Lavena.

ARTHUR: I told you Orage'd be good.

SIS: You did ... thankyou for inviting me.

ARTHUR: Not at all. I think you're smashing, Sis. Do you ... do you ... think...

SIS: I ... have to go now.

ARTHUR: Go where?

SIS: Home.

ARTHUR: Why?

SIS: Why do you think?

ARTHUR: Don't go home. Walk ... with me ... let's talk ... and think more about...

SIS: Ideas!

ARTHUR: Art.

SIS: Possibilities.

ARTHUR: Summer days when we can walk up Castle Hill and think on the Luddites and the Chartists holding rallies there...

19

SIS: And my Grandad holding dogfights and bare knuckle boxing.

ARTHUR: Lot of money made and lost up there. We have a lot of history here and we ought be proud of it ... there's a lot in it for where we are now and ought to be going ... in the future Sis.

SIS: What future? Here we are talking ideas ... while they all scream war in the newspapers.

ARTHUR: Oh they have to go on about something to get you to buy it. Don't fret about all that. We have better things to think on ... you and I.

SIS: What like? I mean I'd like...

ARTHUR: All the things we can do ... things we can make better for people ... so they don't end like Percy's dad, old and done-in at 45 ... but can live like men and women are meant to live ... stand up, part of a world that sees them as more than fodder for factories.

SIS: And cannons.

ARTHUR: We have a lot to do Sis. Come on.

Exit SIS.

SCENE 6

ARTHUR & PERCY *place a soapbox down and get ready to campaign.*

It is summer 1914. St George's Square is bathed in a heady glow of early evening sunlight and the air is thick with horse manure. Wonderful. (*coughs*) Bloody hell...

ARTHUR: What do you reckon, crowd big enough yet? I'm gonna speak tonight about patriotism.

PERCY: (*thinking*) Free love.

ARTHUR: It's a myth.

PERCY: Fancy that, eh?

ARTHUR: Just newspapers pumpin' it out.

PERCY: I do anyway.

ARTHUR: They have a very one sided-view of patriotism these people.

PERCY: Be hell of a thing wouldn't it?

ARTHUR: It's what we have to practice and they get paid for!

PERCY: Do you think it'd catch on round here?

ARTHUR: It's well caught on. Patriotic songs...

PERCY: I mean free love, sod patriotism!

ARTHUR: Free love? Percy for God's sake! It's Europeans pushing all that sort of thing.

PERCY: So? We're *Internationalists* aren't we?

ARTHUR: Not that far we're not. Free love means one thing only.

PERCY: I know!

ARTHUR: A shotgun wedding, and house full of damp nappies.

PERCY: Oh. That's two things!

ARTHUR: Worse still, the *not* so freely loving glances of ones reluctant in-laws!

PERCY: Three! And all of 'em bad! No, no, no.

ARTHUR: No no and thrice no. Our Socialism is spun from the home grown, finest worsted variety.

PERCY: You're right. Hewn from the ancient millstone grit.

ARTHUR: Soaked for centuries in Wesleyan Chapel chastity!

PERCY: You can take the boy out of the Colne Valley.

ARTHUR: But he must keep his vest on.

PERCY: Catch his death, poor sod.

ARTHUR: Besides, how is a feller to stoke up his ideological fires if he's ... been...

PERCY: Stoking up his other ones?

ARTHUR: Amen. Our fellowship must be of the profoundly trousered variety. No question.

PERCY: None at all.

ARTHUR *jumps on the soapbox.*

21

ARTHUR: Brothers, sisters, you've no doubt been reading the newspapers, some feller we've never heard of in Sarajevo's been shot. Aye, shame, very sad and all that, but it's beggar all to do with us, is it? But here we are, being asked to go to war over conflicts in eastern Europe and far afield. It is merely a fight for foreign markets that we are not prepared to give our lives for. It is our business as Socialists to develop a class patriotism, refusing to murder one another for a sordid world capitalism…

PERCY: Arthur watch out … it's getting nasty… Arthur look out!

SCENE 7

Music comes in. Enter LILIAN LENTON. *She strikes and holds a pose in the manner of a dancer, elegant and beautiful. The music ends.*

Enter LILIAN LENTON.

LILIAN: I … am an arsonist! I … am the anti-Christ … I know what I want … and I know how to get it!

Lilian Lenton.

Suffragette,

Dancer,

Window smasher.

And arsonist.

And, if I may say, slim, lithe and strikingly beautiful.

And now, in our story.

SIS: Well thrump my kettle drum we've never had an arsonist at the Socialist Sunday School before! Not a real *proper* one, you know. Wait till Arthur and Percy get here, they will be impressed!

LILIAN: I'm told there is a safe house near here?

SIS: A music shop on Bradford Road, it belongs to a woman called Edith Key. Are you a real, trained dancer?

LILIAN: Yes.

SIS: I would have loved to be a dancer, or an actress.

LILIAN: So why aren't you?

SIS: My father would have been against it.

LILIAN: So? So was mine.

SIS: Really. What did you do?

Music – they begin to dance, LILIAN *leads,* SIS *follows. Enter another actor as* MOTHER.

LILIAN: One day I said, mother…

MOTHER: What dear?

LILIAN: I want to be a dancer.

MOTHER: (*shrieks*) Oh my God! The shame! The shame! Never! Kill me now!

LILIAN: Mother don't over react.

MOTHER: But from the stage to the prostitute's boudoir is barely a hop, skip and a trip! Father – dear Lilian is to become a dancer!

FATHER: What!? Hold still my darling and I'll kill you now.

MOTHER: Thankyou dear.

LILIAN: Suddenly I was swimming in an ocean of radical new ideas, a world that was changing before my eyes, I fell in love…

SIS: Really!? Who with?

LILIAN: Revolutionary dance theatre!

SIS: Gosh. Is he foreign?

LILIAN: Dance!

SIS: I'm trying.

LILIAN: No I fell in love with dance!

SIS: Oh I see, sorry.

LILIAN: Performance that breaks all the rules, that is exciting! Everything I thought I knew … I didn't.

SIS: I bet you're a free lover, aren't you?

LILIAN: (*shocked*) I beg your pardon? Where did you hear of that?

23

Sis: Alfred Orage spoke about it. He spoke of ... other things too ... quite radical.

Lilian: Such as?

Sis: Of love between ... men and...

Lilian: Themselves?

Sis: No ... other ... men. And also women and...

Lilian: Women yes ... it's quite common dear. Men are as trapped in their self-imposed straitjacket as they have us bound and gagged in ours. Then I heard Emmeline Pankhurst speak ... Either women are to be killed or women are to have the vote.

Sis: Can't we just march and make lovely banners?

Lilian: Too late for that. As soon as I was 21 I adopted the nom de plume of Miss Ida Inkley. My first act of militancy was to take part in a great big whopping window smash!

HYMN SINGING – to the sound of smashing windows & raging infernos!

Lilian: My second was to torch Kew Gardens pavilion. Now my aim is to burn two buildings a week.

Sis: A week?

Lilian: I want to prove it is impossible to govern without the consent of the governed. No one can ignore arson.

Sis: No, you can't miss it. But they'll jail you.

Lilian: They already have. I went on hunger strike.

Sis: Oh, are you not normally so slim?

Lilian: I almost died.

Sis: Sorry.

Lilian: They force fed me, passed the pipe into my trachea by accident, pumped some slop into my lung. I was gravely ill, so they released me to get better, but only long enough for me to get some strength back.

Sis: Soon as there's colour in your cheeks, back in?

Lilian: The cat and mouse act. So I went on hunger strike again. They're afraid one of us might die in there, become a martyr to the cause.

Sis: And would you? Become a martyr?

Lilian: I don't know. The more they harangued, bullied, ill-treated me … the stronger my conviction. I forgot everything else … I had no life outside … no past no future … just that cold and dirty cell where so many women before had been caged … one thought only…

Sis: What?

Lilian: That if I broke I'd regret it always, I'd be a failure. Every ounce of my will became about defying them.

Sis: It could have killed you.

Lilian: I thought that everyday. Am I ready to die for this?

Sis: And?

Lilian: No. Of course not. Who ever is? Besides, I'll be far more annoying to them alive and kicking! I'm going to need a disguise, the police are everywhere.

Enter Isaac.

Isaac: Sis. Hello … Miss.

Sis: This is Lilian … no Ida Ink…

Lilian: May Dennis?

Isaac: (*pause*) I don't know, depends what he wants to do.

Lilian: No I'm May Dennis.

Isaac: Oh, I see. Lilian, Ida, May, Dennis make your bloody mind up.

Sis: There's no need to swear.

Isaac: Why not? It's not a flaming church, is it? Socialist 10 commandments? It's blasphemy. So where is he? The little traitor? Off learning German 'appen?

Sis: Please don't start saying things about him again.

Isaac: Recruitment in Huddersfield is way below other towns. It's a civic shame and all his bloody fault, him and Ellis spouting in St George's Square!

Sis: If you say so. Why are you here?

IsAAC: I want you to come home Sis. Your brothers have joined up. West Yorkshire Regiment. They're going to France tomorrow.

SIS: Tomorrow? So soon? I didn't realize ... well ... I just need to finish some things here and I'll be there.

IsAAC: Finish what?

SIS: Just things I have to do, go home dad and I'll be there in a bit.

IsAAC: It's time to stop this. I don't want you running round with Gardiner no more. I'm telling you to come home now.

SIS: You're telling me?

IsAAC: I am. Now get your coat and come on.

SIS: No.

IsAAC: What?

SIS: I will not be told what to do ... by you or anybody else.

IsAAC: Won't you.

IsAAC *takes hold of* SIS's *arm, she tries to pull away he won't let go.*

IsAAC: He's poisoned you with his rotten Socialism! Took you away from your family.

LILIAN: Mr Timmins ... let go of her arm.

IsAAC: What the hell's it got to do with you?

SIS: Please Lil ... Ida ... May ... I'll deal with it.

IsAAC: Sis don't do this. To your brothers.

SIS: I love my brothers.

IsAAC: But what? You hate me ... is that what they've done to you?

SIS: I just don't agree with this war ... it's all about the profits, markets.

IsAAC: That's Gardiner talking, not you.

SIS: What about the Quakers, they are refusing to fight too. What about them? Why don't you hate them as much?

IsAAC: That's different.

SIS: How?

26

ISAAC: They believe in God. Gardiner, Ellis ... what do they believe in?

SIS: People.

ISAAC: People? They'll be sadly disappointed there. They'll shoot the likes of Gardiner, you know. I hope they do.

SIS: And if they do ... I'll never forgive you for saying that. And you'll never see me again.

Exit ISAAC.

SIS: They won't shoot him ... will they?

LILIAN: This war's a disaster. Setting families against each other. It's going to split the women's movement, just as we're about to get real change. What do we need a war for? Who does it serve? Certainly not half the population but then we don't get any say in the matter, do we!

SIS: No we just get to pick up the pieces. Oh, now look at the boat I'm in!

Enter ARTHUR *and* PERCY *nursing wounds.*

SIS: What's happened?

ARTHUR: We copped it in town.

PERCY: Again.

ARTHUR: Big ugly squaddie, with a face like a steam engine at full throttle hit me with a lead pipe. I got him back, mind.

LILIAN: What's your name?

PERCY: Percy. What's yours?

LILIAN: May Dennis. Take your clothes off.

PERCY: What!? Oh I see ... well, as it happens I am versed in the arts of free love, so yes if you're...

LILIAN: And put mine on.

PERCY: Woah! Arthur what about this, eh!? I'm game if you are...

ARTHUR: It's to help her escape, Percy. The police are watching, they're all over.

LILIAN: From the safe house here I'm to be taken to Harrogate, from there I will be transported to Scarborough, and from there to

Holland. Goodbye Sis. Don't be put off from what you believe in.

SIS: Goodbye Lilian ... Ida ... May ... Dennis...

PERCY *and* LILIAN *exit.* SIS *tends* ARTHUR'S *wounds.*

Ladies and gentlemen – Lilian Lenton. After leaving a trail of destruction and living on the run for two years, Lilian went to Serbia, where she served as a nurse for the remaining years of the war. She remained a formidable figure in the Women's movement for the rest of her days.

SIS: Pacifism has a funny habit of starting a lot of fights.

ARTHUR: We can't be put off by things like that. Bust my finger on that bloke's thick head!

SIS: It's broken ... and you've a black eye coming up ... bruised lip.

She inspects him closely, intimately.

ARTHUR: I want us, me and thee, to get wed, Sis.

SIS: *(pause)* Give over.

ARTHUR: I aren't the type to give over. Well?

SIS: Since I've met you I've thought about things in a way I never thought possible.

ARTHUR: I see. And one of them is whether you want to get married? Or just to me, is that?

SIS: My father talks of my brothers going to the front ... and look what I'm doing.

ARTHUR: You're doing what's right, Sis.

SIS: I wonder if I am though.

ARTHUR: Don't weaken now Sis ... don't turn again us ... I couldn't stand that. For all the support we have ... every day I'm called a traitor, a coward, or is that what you think as well?

SIS: No, of course not.

ARTHUR: Then marry me!

SIS: No. I will not just do somebody else's bidding! That's been my whole

life ... doing things to please everybody else ... made to feel like
I'm...

ARTHUR: Great. I've opened your eyes so wide ... that you now see
straight past me? Is it not what you want as well?

SIS: If you're sent to France ... and refuse to fight ... I'll be a widow
before I've put the wedding frock away ... and I couldn't stand that. I
need to go home, see my brothers off.

Exit SIS.

SCENE 8

Enter JOHN HUNTER WATTS.

The year of 1916 approaches. Into our play comes Mr John Hunter
Watts ... a stalwart of the British Socialist movement.

WATTS: I know.

I'm telling them, not you. Stalwart of the British Socialist movement
since the 1880s.

Enter ARTHUR.

WATTS: Arthur ... good to see you young man.

ARTHUR: Mr Hunter Watts. We are honoured in Huddersfield. I didn't
expect to see you in this district.

WATTS: I hear you're doing fine things for the union ... we need lads like
you. Fire in their belly.

ARTHUR: We've got the whole of the Labour and Socialist movement in
Huddersfield united agin the war.

WATTS: So you lads are making a stir. They make fully one third of the
explosives used by the army right here in Huddersfield.

ARTHUR: British Dyes, Holliday & Son as well.

WATTS: I was asked to come here ... pay you all a visit.

ARTHUR: Who by? Mr Brockway? Bertrand Russell?

WATTS: The War Office.

ARTHUR: The War office?

29

WATTS: It seems the deepest strain of opposition to recruiting comes from this district.

ARTHUR: There is a very strong pacifist element here.

WATTS: What is it in this town? Is there something in the water? Breeds this little band of Quaker anarchists and anti-patriotic pacifists?

ARTHUR: In the blood, not water. What are you saying Mr Watts?

WATTS: I shall be establishing a Workers Own Recruitment Committee.

ARTHUR: You?

WATTS: I'm placing an advert in The Clarion, for men to form a Pals company for Socialists.

ARTHUR: You'll not get many.

WATTS: Socialists ... and Patriots.

ARTHUR: Shame on you. We have Liberals, Labour, ILP, church and layman against this war ... now you come here to support it?

WATTS: Because I believe it's right. Even Mrs Pankhurst agrees.

ARTHUR: Her daughter doesn't. Sylvia. What about her?

WATTS: The British worker is convinced he is fighting a noble cause, against an evil adversary.

ARTHUR: So am I.

WATTS: Arthur you're not helping the Socialist cause, you're poisoning it. We need practical plans ... skilful manoeuvres. This war is a necessary thing. We have to fight it, us, the working class ... to stop the German advance.

ARTHUR: What do we lose by that?

WATTS: But what do we *gain*, by winning it? The workers will benefit, we'll get progress and real change ... stuff we've been fighting years for. But if you keep this up, we'll be holed below the waterline forever. People won't trust us to defend the national interest.

ARTHUR: Real change, you say. Such as?

WATTS: Schools, hospitals, sanitation...

ARTHUR: How? They're spending billions on weapons ... two million

30

quid a day on bullets ... they'll be in debt for years. We won't get nothing, Mr Watts. Nothing! This war is no concern of the working class.

WATTS: I read the Socialist newspapers too.

ARTHUR: And their duty to themselves is to take every advantage of such lapses into insanity by the capitalist class.

WATTS: It's easy to write things like that. The other day I passed by one of your gatherings.

ARTHUR: Should have stayed and listened.

WATTS: And I thought ... in any other country in Europe those men's lives would not be worth five minutes purchase. They would have been kicked from hell to Halifax, dragged through the streets – skunks, scoundrels, cowards, pacifists, neuters, neither men nor women. In Scotland such a meeting would be impossible, in London and Liverpool it would be impossible, in almost any other country it would be impossible. But here ... it is ... why?

ARTHUR: Cos people here aren't daft. This Colne Valley ... you walk past old fellers, whose old fellers spilt blood in the Luddite rising ... they had more soldiers here than they had at Waterloo, did you know that?

WATTS: It's history. 100 years ago, we need to look forward not back.

ARTHUR: Folk here are proud of that history. It's their own, not a fairytale handed down about kings and queens ... that's the history that keeps 'em captive ... this is another that sets 'em free, real solid history, dug, scraped and clawed out of the earth, engineered, woven, designed and built from the bottom up ... one small piece everyday by people risking their lives to change the world they lived in, like we are now, inch by back breaking inch ... that, Mr Watts is what's in the water here.

WATTS: And you've created this little hotbed of pacifism? I believe it to be a mistake. Some of the employers locally have agreed to ... release men from their labours.

ARTHUR: *Release?* Sack them? So they have no option but sign up?

WATTS: Those who do will have their jobs held open.

ARTHUR: It's compulsory voluntaryism ... conscription!

WATTS: It's the best way to avoid it!

31

ARTHUR: Call yourself a Socialist?

WATTS: I do. And I'm proud of it, people like me and Robert Blatchford. And come the peace, we'll make a whole new contract with employers ... the war is a good thing for us!

ARTHUR: You're asking me to betray everything I believe in. Never.

WATTS: The Earl of Derby's Scheme is the last hope for voluntaryism. Then it's Conscription.

ARTHUR: They'll have to make allowance for those who object ... whose conscience won't permit it.

WATTS: Decent God-fearing folks maybe. But not you, Arthur. You'll just be law breakers. Arrested. Forced to serve. Once you get to France ... it's fight ... or the firing squad. Shot as cowards.

ARTHUR: You see that Mr Watts (*holds his crooked finger up*) it's permanently crooked. I got it punching a soldier, after he hit me with a lead pipe. I aren't scared.

WATTS: Tell it to the Tribunal.

SCENE 9 – THE TRIBUNAL

ARTHUR *readies himself for the Tribunal. The remaining cast enter, one by one, introduce themselves, and take their seat.*

Huddersfield Town Hall, March 20th, 1916. A large number of cases of conscientious objection to military service are to be heard. So large is the public attendance that the crowd extends into the corridors and when the name of Arthur Gardiner is called...

There is now a burst of clapping and cheering, through which we hear...

The Huddersfield Military Service Tribunal will now sit ... comprising...

ARMITAGE: Respected local businessman Mr W H Armitage.

BLAMIRES: The Mayor of Huddersfield Mr J Blamires,

CROSLAND: The military representative Mr A P Crosland.

PICKLES: And lastly Mr J Pickles, Labour member and textile worker.

BLAMIRES: After that unseemly demonstration I am minded to clear the court and we will hear this case in private!

PICKLES: As far as I am aware there was no pre-arrangement to applaud Arthur Gardiner, who is a very popular man in the Socialist movement. I hope that in the public interest the Mayor will overlook the applause and reverse the decision.

ARTHUR: To remove any doubt the Tribunal may have, personally I was more surprised than the members of the Tribunal. There has been nothing whatever arranged. Perhaps I can account for the applause and the demonstration because I have taken up a definite anti-war attitude in times of peace as well as war.

Hear hear...

CROSLAND: It has nothing to do with Mr Gardiner. The crowd are misbehaving themselves.

PICKLES: It is not misbehaviour Mr Mayor but a case of very strong feeling which should not prejudice the applicant.

BLAMIRES: We are here in a very difficult position doing our best. (*laughter*)

PICKLES: They have not taken up any antagonism to you or the tribunal. They want to hear the case. As citizens they have a right to speak.

BLAMIRES: I will not have any further discussion.

PICKLES: We will be here all night then. It is not a fair trial if it is in private.

Shouts of Free Speech, Free Speech!

ARTHUR: I understood the Tribunal was a court of Justice and not an autocratic assembly (*Applause*) as we boast so much of British Liberty, why not give fair play? You say you are going against German methods, and yet you are adopting them.

BLAMIRES: I have made my appeal for these people to retire. Now you shall make yours. On the first interruption I shall refuse to go on with the case, and you agree to go into another room to hear the case.

ARTHUR: Women and men – I appeal to you that no further demonstration shall take place during the hearing of my case. If justice is not meted out to me and my comrades, I put it to you as an individual, that I do not count. I am simply here as the trustee of the opinions

33

and conscientious objections of the men of different parties and organisations who have principles like I have and hold the international solidarity of the workers should be placed before anything else. Because I want fair play and no favours, I ask you that no interjections of interruptions of any kind whatever shall take place while I am on my trial. (*Cheer*)

BLAMIRES: You are not on trial.

ARTHUR: I think I am.

BLAMIRES: On what basis do you claim exemption?

ARTHUR: I am 26 years of age, and employed as a wool and cotton dyer. I cannot conscientiously undertake combatant or non-combatant military service. For a number of years I have devoted my time and energy both publicly and privately, to the economic and moral upliftment of humanity. I am opposed to all forms of militarism, believing it to be detrimental to the welfare of nations.

CROSLAND: Can you produce any evidence to show that this belief is not of recent date?

ARTHUR: Yes, I can produce sufficient evidence to convince this Tribunal. I could produce women and men to show that for many years I have advocated anti-militarist views and the sacredness of human life.

CROSLAND: You are against militarism. I am against it too, and always have been. That is no reason why you should not go to fight for your country.

ARTHUR: I have no country.

CROSLAND: What are you doing here, having no country? Why are you receiving all the benefits of a citizen when you have no country?

ARTHUR: Whatever benefits I am receiving have only been got by the organised workers wringing them from the master class. I am here this afternoon defending one of the liberties we at present enjoy, the liberty of conscience.

CROSLAND: Can I suggest non-combatant service?

BLAMIRES: He objects to combatant and to non-combatant, and he objects on conscientious grounds.

ARTHUR: My objection is not only to killing another but also to making ammunition.

BLAMIRES: You don't object to shelter here behind the brave men who are fighting?

ARTHUR: I am quite prepared to leave the country if you allow me to do so.

CROSLAND: There are people who would be very glad to get rid of you if you would pay your own expenses.

ARTHUR: I am prepared to pay my own expenses if you will allow me to leave the country.

BLAMIRES: You might getting "out of the frying pan and into the fire". What country would you go to?

ARTHUR: I don't think I should tell the Tribunal. It is immaterial which country I would go to.

BLAMIRES: Go to Germany perhaps?

ARTHUR: Perhaps so. I might not be any worse off than I am here.

CROSLAND: I think you are talking through your hat.

ARTHUR: That is a matter of opinion.

CROSLAND: This conscientious objection is an unsubstantial thing.

ARTHUR: No, conscience is a material thing. You might not be able to understand it, other people perhaps can.

BLAMIRES: "The economic and moral upliftment of humanity…"

ARTHUR: That is so; German as well as Britisher.

BLAMIRES: I don't know what you are going to do.

ARTHUR: The Tribunal agrees with me, it is a noble ideal and I ask to be allowed to do it and go into highways and byways and get the people to my opinion. That is the way to settle wars.

BLAMIRES: You can convince the people in time of peace, but when their blood is up you will have to do something to stop it, and only by physical means can you do it.

ARTHUR: You can never kill militarism by militarism.

35

BLAMIRES: Your movement is in a minority.

ARTHUR: All movements start from minorities. Minorities are going to settle the war; the people are not going to settle the war. If you would leave it to them, it would have been settled long since.

BLAMIRES: The people of this country are acting through the Government.

ARTHUR: Yes, and the government are a minority.

BLAMIRES: And you are a minority who are opposing the considered action of your own representatives.

ARTHUR: That action does not settle that the minority is wrong.

BLAMIRES: But it is a fact. There is a minority in Germany probably. It is all dependent on physical force.

ARTHUR: I cannot accept that. If Germany licks us by physical force, do you think the militarists in this country will be content? I realize the interests of the workers of Germany are identical with those of the workers of England, and for that reason I cannot march against them and will not.

CROSLAND: And you will not do non-combatant service?

ARTHUR: Certainly not.

BLAMIRES: They are fighting against England!

ARTHUR: No, they are not fighting against me.

BLAMIRES: Well you are a unit in this empire.

ARTHUR: No; I don't think my name has been brought up at all in the Reichstag.

BLAMIRES: It would have been absurd to do so.

ARTHUR: Certainly it would. It is not my fault that I was born here. I am neither to be praised nor blamed for it.

BLAMIRES: But you are fortunate that you were born here.

ARTHUR: That may be.

BLAMIRES:Well, I am glad you admit so much. Well, are the Tribunal satisfied?

36

ARMITAGE: He objects to one as well as the other. I should refuse it, sir.

PICKLES: I think Mr Gardiner has made a splendid case.

ARMITAGE: But he has such curious ideas. They can't be worked.

PICKLES: I should like to ask the Town Clerk if this Tribunal has the power to grant him exemption on conscientious grounds.

ARTHUR: Mr Armitage says I have curious views. Because you do not agree with them does not mean I do not hold those views.

CROSLAND: This case is not different from the other cases.

BLAMIRES: I think he has proved consistency in his experience. That is rather different from the others. I have a feeling we might…

CROSLAND: What sect do you belong to?

ARTHUR: I am an atheist.

BLAMIRES: Have Atheists consciences do you think?

ARTHUR: Oh yes! I am a member of the British Socialist Party and a member of the Socialist Sunday School.

CROSLAND: I should refuse it. Whatever you do I shall oppose your decision.

BLAMIRES: That won't make the slightest difference.

CROSLAND: It seems so foreign to have a man talk as he does.

BLAMIRES: I think I should like to retire.

The Tribunal all rise. ARTHUR *sits. The Tribunal are now in their private rooms.*

BLAMIRES: What the blazes are we supposed to do with this feller? He's not going to budge an inch is he?

CROSLAND: Have him shot, that's what!

PICKLES: As the law stands a man can appeal for absolute exemption on grounds of conscience. Gardiner has proved that his claim is based on clear conscientious grounds. Therefore we should grant him exemption.

CROSLAND: We can't! If we grant this to Gardiner it will set a precedent and how many more will there be?

ARMITAGE: But the man has made his case. What do we do?

BLAMIRES: I have no idea.

CROSLAND: Refuse it!

PICKLES: Grant it.

BLAMIRES: We'll have to send it to a higher court. We can't grant him exemption on political grounds, I agree with Mr Crosland, what will happen to the entire war effort? We'll end up with chaos.

ARTHUR *stands up once more. The Tribunal resume their seats.*

BLAMIRES: Well ... we have had some difficulty in coming to a decision, however we have decided by a majority that we believe that the applicant is entitled to call himself a conscientious objector.

We are very sorry that a man of his attainments and ability cannot see the interests of this country at the present time are in an opposite direction, but in view of the fact that we believe in the sincerity of his convictions, we are disposed to grant temporary exemption for two months. Which could carry to four months.

ARTHUR: I cannot accept the decision. I suppose I shall have the right of appeal?

BLAMIRES: That is what we want. We want this case considered.

SCENE 10

SIS *approaches* ARTHUR.

SIS: You ran rings round 'em! What's more they accepted the case ... exemption on political grounds.

ARTHUR: For two months.

SIS: I have no country ... their faces when you said that! A picture!

ARTHUR: When everyone cheered, Blamires and Crosland looked at me ... I could see it ... shivers running down their spine.

SIS: What will happen after two months?

ARTHUR: We'll get our call-up papers. And if we still refuse to fight, we'll get two years hard labour. At best.

SIS: They won't grant exemption on political grounds?

ARTHUR: How can they? The whole war would collapse. Half the lads out there'd drop their gun and walk off the job just like they ought to.

SIS: But you won! They couldn't beat your argument ... now they know, like we do, that when they talk about defending democracy and freedom it's a fiction.

ARTHUR: Aye.

SIS: What? What's wrong?

ARTHUR: Some friends in the union have put me in touch with a bloke in Liverpool, a Sinn Feiner, he's in the coal trimmers union.

SIS: So?

ARTHUR: He can get us union cards.

SIS: What to ... to get on the boats?

ARTHUR: And help get others onto 'em, Sinn Feiners, suffragettes, COs like us.

SIS: The boats ... to where?

ARTHUR: America. It's the best thing to do.

SIS: America?

ARTHUR: They're trying to launch the war over there as well ... we can do a lot of good out there I reckon.

SIS *doesn't speak for some time.*

ARTHUR: I asked you to marry me Sis.

SIS: Good job I didn't.

ARTHUR: What do you want me to do? What have I got to stay here for? I'm looking at two years hard labour ... or worse, the firing squad in France ... or America ... where I can make a difference. We have work to do Sis.

SIS: Here, not in America! Or when you said you had no country did that really mean that?! No, you're right. Go. Who am I to stop you. I'm sorry.

ARTHUR: Please, Sis ... I'd give anything to see you walk down the aisle to me.

SIS: But it's not to be and there it is. And why should it? Everyday another list in the newspaper ... all the dead ones ... people take their caps off, say how sad but he died doing his duty ... proves how loyal they are. Heck, now that the neighbours have sacrificed their son, come on Mrs Jones, least you can do is send yours! It's madness, I don't want to get married and have children ... for this.

ARTHUR: I'll come back.

SIS: No you won't. You'll be a deserter. From the army. From the cause. From me. Take care.

SIS *exits.*

ARTHUR: Sis ...?

SCENE 11

ARTHUR *and* PERCY *at Otley Chevin.*

PERCY: You got your call up papers?

ARTHUR: Aye. You?

PERCY: Came yesterday. America, I've always dreamed of it.

ARTHUR: Not half ... skyscrapers ... moving picture palaces.

PERCY: You won't see Sis again.

ARTHUR: Old Isaac'll dance through George's Square won't he?

PERCY: Roar his socks off ... 'I told thee he were nowt but a shiverin' bloody...

PERCY *stops himself. Each looks at the other.*

ARTHUR: Aye. A coward and a wet livered shirker.

PERCY: Everything they've said about us.

ARTHUR: Neither men ... nor women.

PERCY: Let 'em say what they want. We don't need to prove how tough we are to anyone.

ARTHUR: No. Course not. Percy ... you go.

PERCY: What about you?

ARTHUR: I'm not giving old man Timmins the satisfaction. I might not be able to come back ... see her again. Wouldn't matter if I lived or died anyway then.

PERCY: If we finish up in France ... they're doing it to lads that desert. Won't blink an eye over us will they?

ARTHUR: No.

PERCY: It's a funny thing to think about ... looking at firing squad.

ARTHUR: I can't imagine it ... what it must be like for 'em. Poor sods. Go to America Percy, I want you to go.

PERCY: No. I'm not going without you. No matter what Arthur. If you stay strong, and face it ... if it comes ... so will I. I promise.

ARTHUR: You're a good lad, Percy. The best mate a bloke could have.

SCENE 12

ARTHUR *and* PERCY *are arrested.*

Stirring sendoff at railway station, Saturday October 7th, 1916.

A military uniform is handed to ARTHUR. *He refuses to touch it.*

Ellis, Gardiner, to be court martialled for their refusal to put on army uniform.

Following Gardiner's performance before the Tribunal, The Justices of The Kings Bench have clarified that a Conscientious Objector's only right is to refuse combatant service.

ARTHUR *addresses the crowd.*

ARTHUR: I do not want to be placed in the position of an outlaw and law-breaker, but I will accept the position gladly rather than obey laws which would force me to act against my principles and beliefs.

PERCY: We are Absolutists and will lift not one finger for this war.

Before the train left Huddersfield The Red Flag was sung, followed by hearty cheers for the prisoners and their principles as they were taken to Halifax, and from there to Rugely Barracks, South Staffordshire.

The singing ends. ARTHUR *and* PERCY *leave.* SIS *is joined by* LAVENA.

SIS: It feels like they have gone off to war.

LAVENA: At least they're alive, and not lost forever.

SIS: Don't say that, my brothers are over there. Least you don't have anyone there.

LAVENA: I might have.

SIS: How come?

LAVENA: I've met someone.

SIS: Oh? As in ... *met* ... *someone?*

LAVENA: His name's George. He's a soldier. He's been over there ... says it has to be done. I've told him where I stand.

SIS: What did he say?

LAVENA: He agrees. But he says he can't let all his mates down. He's very kind ... and good ... he bought me tea in the Midland Hotel in Bradford and asked me.

SIS: Asked you what?

LAVENA: To marry him.

SIS: Never? Oh sorry, I didn't mean it like that, I just thought you weren't the marrying kind.

LAVENA: I told him I won't be giving up my political work to wash vests and longjohns.

SIS: Or to clean doorsteps and sideboard covers.

LAVENA: No.

SIS: Oh no.

LAVENA: No.

Both No!

LAVENA: I said George.

SIS *now adopts her impression of George.*

SIS: Aye lass?

LAVENA: You've to take me as I am.

SIS: Aye, I reckon so … still 'n all tha's reet enough.

LAVENA: Because George.

SIS: What lass?

LAVENA: I only pass through this world once, and I don't intend to pass through as a bird flies through the air, leaving no track behind.

SIS: I wudna want thee to.

LAVENA: There are plenty of people plodding along beaten tracks without my joining the company. There are miles and miles of little frequented path's on life's highway and faintly marked pathways always attracted me more than the beaten road.

SIS: Aye. Lavena.

LAVENA: What George?

SIS drops impression of George.

SIS: You're moving to Bradford. Arthur's gone to prison. Where's that leave me? I will see you again won't I? I aren't losing you as well am I?

LAVENA: No of course not. Don't worry about that Sis.

SIS: Some people don't speak to me anymore … must be hard when they fret about their son or husband over there … others come up and treat me like I'm something special … I feel a bit of a fraud.

LAVENA: You are something special. Without you he wouldn't be able to do it.

SIS: Arthur? Don't worry about him. Nothing'll put him off his stride. I worry about Percy though.

LAVENA: I'll send you a wedding invite.

SIS: Oh please do. I'm happy for you.

LAVENA: Right, I've to be off. Meeting in Dewsbury.

SIS: Votes for Women!

Lavena Saltonstall continued her work through the Workers Education Association throughout the rest of her days. In 1917 she married George Baker and moved to Bradford. She died in 1957.

SCENE 13

ARTHUR *is forcibly ragged out of his jacket, trousers, shoes, down to his longjohns and vest. Army uniform is physically thrust onto him. He does nothing to assist or resist.*

OFFICER: Name?

ARTHUR: Arthur Gardiner.

OFFICER: Age?

ARTHUR: 26.

OFFICER: Married or single?

ARTHUR: Single.

OFFICER: What's your religion?

ARTHUR: Agnostic.

OFFICER: I want your religion not your bloody nationality!

ARTHUR: Agnostic.

OFFICER: Well how do you spell it?

ARTHUR: A. G. N. O. S. T. I. C.

OFFICER: And what's it mean?

ARTHUR: Means you should have studied at school and you'd be able to spell.

ARTHUR *is knocked to the ground.*

OFFICER: Plate, knife, fork, spoon, pint mug, salt jar, slate and pencil … Welcome to Wormwood Scrubs. You get one letter a month but none for the first two months, give you a little time to reflect won't it?

ARTHUR: Should do shouldn't it?

OFFICER: Shut it. Oh, nearly forgot, you get a book as well. A bible.

ARTHUR: Bible's no good to me.

OFFICER: Keep it shut. We have a rule of Silence here. Just like in church. Oh, but you're Agnostic … so instead of chapel of a Sunday you get to clean the shithouses.

ARTHUR: Fine by me, old pal.

OFFICER: Shuttup! And it's sir! Every time you speak to an officer or superior you say sir. Understand?

ARTHUR: Yes.

OFFICER: Yes what?

ARTHUR: Yes, I understand. Long as you understand I'm not in the army, so I don't have to call you sir.

OFFICER: You just won't shuttup will you?

ARTHUR: No.

OFFICER: No what?

ARTHUR: No I just won't shuttup.

OFFICER: Didn't you go to school?

ARTHUR: Yes.

OFFICER: Yes what?

ARTHUR: Yes, I went to school.

OFFICER: Didn't they learn you any manners?

ARTHUR: Yes.

OFFICER: Yes what?

ARTHUR: Yes, they learnt me manners.

OFFICER: Yes, they learnt me manners, sir! Well I'm about to learn you some more.

ARTHUR *is knocked to the floor, and left there.*

Don't worry old pal, you'll break. They all do. One feller ended up crying for his mammy inside a week.

SCENE 14

The other cast members clear the stage leaving ARTHUR *and* PERCY *alone. Both are now visibly knocked about.*

ARTHUR: You alright Percy?

PERCY: Yeah. (*pause*) No. Four of 'em knocked hell out of me. Dragged me round a field ... punching me ... kept throwing a kitbag at me ...

45

pinned me arms back, near wrenched 'em out of their socket. I can't move this one right.

ARTHUR: Same. It's only what we expected.

PERCY: Fancy a game of draughts?

ARTHUR: What with?

PERCY: We'll draw a board out ... and use bits of bread crusts and bacon rind for pieces.

ARTHUR: You're a genius.

They scratch out the board, placing bits of bread for pieces. Enter a soldier. He watches them, mimes loading his gun and shooting the two of them.

OFFICER: Attention!

ARTHUR *and* PERCY *ignore him.*

ARTHUR: It's your move, Percy.

OFFICER: Stand up the pair of you!

PERCY *moves his draughts.*

ARTHUR: Cagey.

OFFICER: Get up. Before I drag you up.

They both stand up, slowly.

ARTHUR: Now, what are you wanting?

OFFICER: To know something. What is you hate so much about this country?

ARTHUR: I don't hate this country, brother. I love it. Specially that Colne Valley ... It's home. I'd be a fish out of water anywhere else.

OFFICER: I am not your brother. If I had my way I'd blow you from the mouth of a cannon.

He flicks his gloves across ARTHUR'S *face.*

OFFICER: That's what I'd do. Then I'd pick up all the little pieces ... and I'd do it again. Coward. Shirker. Traitor.

He flicks the gloves across ARTHUR'S *face again.* ARTHUR *goes for him, there is a melee.*

Get him away from me! I'll shoot him and be proud to do it.

They close in around him, create a real sense that he is being beaten up.

OFFICER: This man will now do parade. If his conscience doesn't permit him to march, then he is to be force marched.

ARTHUR *doesn't move. Music underscores this.*

OFFICER: Quick march!

A kitbag is thrown at him, it knocks him off his feet. He is dragged back upright.

OFFICER: March him round the field, through full drill. Left right left right...

ARTHUR *is hauled around, arms out wide. His physical wellbeing and health is being battered. His voice rises in intensity on account of the suffering he is enduring.*

ARTHUR: Gentlemen I am charged with "when on active service disobeying a lawful command, given by my superior officer". I plead NOT GUILTY, as I do not acknowledge that I am a soldier, and therefore do not recognize "superior officers". I have refused to obey the order that was given me on conscientious grounds.

OFFICER: If he won't vault over the horse like other soldiers in His Majesty's Army, throw him over it, headfirst. Might not knock some sense into him.

ARTHUR: I have for the last 10 years held deep rooted opinions and convictions in regard to militarism and warfare. I am an International Socialist and anti-Militarist, believing that militarism and war are opposed to the best interest of all nations. I believe modern wars to be the direct outcome of the ridiculous, inhuman and anarchical system of production and distribution under which we live.

OFFICER: Do it again the day after. And then again, and again. Don't make him too comfy in between. He might get used to it.

ARTHUR: I am, and have been for a few years, both scholar and teacher at the Huddersfield Socialist Sunday School, one of whose 10 precepts reads as follows: Do not think that he who loves his own country must hate and despise other nations or wish for war, which is a remnant of barbarism.

OFFICER: He'll break. They all do. Take him round again.

ARTHUR: I am also a member of the No Conscription Fellowship, of whose activities you will no doubt be aware. I mention these few facts in order that you may see that I am sincere and conscientious in my opinions, and in order that you may more clearly understand the reason for my refusal to obey a military order.

He falls to the floor, exhausted.

SCENE 15

ARTHUR *is hauled up before the Governor again.*

Gardiner, Ellis. Seems you've been singing songs in your cell ... you two just can't keep quiet can you?

ARTHUR: No.

Six days dark cells. Get them out of here.

ARTHUR *and* PERCY *are removed to the dark cell. They sit alone, light comes in on him.*

SIS *reads from the letter she has written to* ARTHUR –

Sis Dear Arthur,

I hope this finds you in good spirits. Things are a lot quieter round here without you and Percy, but you are doing the right thing you and we are all very proud of you. There was a meeting at the Victoria Hall the other night and Phillip Snowden the MP spoke. He mentioned you and Percy and said how proud we should be of you and I was ... I am.

Next thing a load of soldiers kicked and fought their way in to the meeting ... 20 or more, to disrupt and attack Mr Snowden and him not a well man, disgusting. They looked so angry ... to hate us so much ... it turned into a proper pitched battle. I was thinking if Arthur were here he'd be right in the middle of this, there were old fellers attacking them with walking sticks and ladies hitting them with brollies, it was just like the wrestling! And people started singing the Red Flag and then the bobbies came!

My brothers keep writing from France. Thankfully nothing awful has happened to either of them. Yet. Father and I virtually don't speak.

Do you remember Tom Whitehead? He was a CO like you ... until he

48

gave in ... after all the pressure that was put on him and things people said I suppose ... I hope they're pleased, because he has been killed in France. I saw his mother the day before yesterday in town.

Miss Robson, you know the family, Quakers, lovely people, Liberal in their politics, she stopped me in the street, I was feeling so miserable ... and she said she was proud of you and Percy and ... I confess I cried. If one person has said that to me hundreds have. Oh, 3000 women marched through Bradford against the war! Lavena was one of them. People on the street clapped and cheered them. There's demonstrations in London and all over the country now, this revolution in Russia's made everyone sit up alright. They've arrested poor Alice Wheeldon in Derby and accused her of a plot to poison Lloyd George! Have you ever heard anything as daft? It's like the whole country's like a cat on hot tin, they're scared Arthur, they are ... just like you and Percy said, folk will see it, it stands to reason!

More and more people say you lads were right all along so be sure and keep your chin up. It's so awful reading the names of the dead ones everyday, to see how many you know ... knew ... I don't open the papers any more. What a country we have become.

She seals the letter and it is handed across the stage through hands until it reaches the OFFICER. *Who looks at then puts it in his pocket.* ARTHUR *never sees it.*

ARTHUR *begins to struggle mentally.* PERCY *begins a set of routine exercises, sit ups, press ups, walking from side to side of his cell. Then he begins calculations in his head. We do not hear what he is doing.*

The following words, spoken, each other cast member takes a line each in turn.

No light. Pitch dark.

You won't know whether it's Christmas or Whitsuntide...

Starts to do things to a feller's mind...

So imagine what it'll do to a slacker like you.

You lose all idea of time, day or night,

Can't see your hand in front of your face.

You think hours have gone by...

But it's only minutes...

You don't hear a sound either…

Except your own weaselly thoughts…

Lightless … soundless…

It's like being dead.

After a while…

You'll wish you were.

Each begins to sing England, Arise! *– ARTHUR struggles to remember the words, but Percy gets stronger and stronger as it goes along.*

ARTHUR: Sis …? Percy …? Who's there? Who is it? Who spoke then? Anyone!? Is anyone there? Someone … anyone … Percy …? Percy! Where are you Percy!? It's me! Me … Arthur? Who's that?

He starts to think, and to compose a letter in his head.

Dear Sis,

I write to you … with … news … from nowhere…

ARTHUR *growing more desperate:*

ARTHUR: No light in here Sis. Pitch dark. You don't know whether it's Christmas or Whitsuntide … starts to do things to a feller's mind … you lose all idea of time, day or night, can't see your hand in front of your face. You think hours have gone by but it's only minutes … you don't hear a sound either … except your own thoughts … round and round … lightless … soundless … it's like being dead. After a while … you wish you were. Sis…

Enter the OFFICER.

OFFICER: Gardiner!

ARTHUR: What time is it? What day is it? Where am I?

OFFICER: Wormwood Scrubs.

ARTHUR: Where's Percy?

OFFICER: Gone.

ARTHUR: Gone? Gone where?

OFFICER: Gone where … sir.

ARTHUR: (*despairing*) Gone where ... sir.

Music begins – sad, emotional, it builds.

OFFICER: To the camp. I told you ... Do you agree to the Home Office Scheme ... to undertake non-combatant duties?

ARTHUR: I am a Socialist, a pacifist. I will not lift one finger to assist in this war.

I do not want to be placed in the position of an outlaw and lawbreaker, but I will accept the position gladly rather than obey laws which would force me to act against my principles and beliefs.

I do not in any way regret any action I have taken, nor do I withdraw any word I have said, and my only hope is that I shall retain sufficient strength, physically and mentally, to go on fighting for the emancipation of the class to which I belong.

OFFICER: Very well.

ARTHUR: I believe in a fellowship ... a brotherhood and sisterhood...

OFFICER: Put him back in the dark cells.

ARTHUR: What? No! You can't! I've done my six days!

OFFICER: No you haven't ... you've only done three ... only half way through.

ARTHUR: What? I can't have ... no ... don't put me back in there.

OFFICER: Take him back down.

ARTHUR: No! Please! Don't ... please ... I ... I can't go back in there ... don't do that...

OFFICER: What's that? Well, do you accept the Home Office Scheme? It's very simple. Yes or no?

ARTHUR*'s head drops. He breaks, crumples to the floor in tears.*

OFFICER: Well? (*no response*) So be it ... take him down.

ARTHUR: (*crying*) No ... don't...

OFFICER: You'll go?

ARTHUR *nods slowly. The music ends.*

51

OFFICER: Good. All we ask is that you pull your weight ... one way or the other. We can't let you people thumb your nose at us. Where will it end you see? We'll stop at nothing.

SCENE 16

PERCY *stands centre stage.*

OFFICER: Ellis. Another traitor ... you people should be hung. Your mate ... Gardiner.

PERCY: What about him?

OFFICER: No spine for the fight ... didn't take him long to snap.

PERCY: Arthur?

OFFICER: Gone to the work camp.

PERCY: Never.

OFFICER: It's true. Well, what do you have to say for yourself?

PERCY: This war's been going since August 1914. As of now that is 952 days. I have heard that 3 million pounds a day is spent on bullets alone.

OFFICER: Have you really?

PERCY: 952 x 3 million is 2 billion 856 million pounds. The other costs of keeping an army in the field, transport, equipment, food, hospital and medical supplies will no doubt be more than double this but since I don't have access to sufficiently accurate figures let's just stick to bullets shall we...

OFFICER: Oh you're a proper one aren't you?

PERCY: The population of Great Britain is at present roughly 42.5 million people though of course that is dropping sharply with each day that passes in France, now if we divide 2 billion 856 million by 42.5 million we arrive at a figure £67 and 5 shillings. For that we could get every family in the country a brand new house with a bath and toilet indoors, we could have new schools, proper hospitals, pensions for the old folks,

OFFICER: Take him back down!

PERCY: Sanitation, free doctors that people aren't scared to call because they can't afford to pay for it…

OFFICER: You make me sick.

PERCY: I feel pretty sick myself, old pal. This war is not a workers matter in its origin, is not a workers matter in its conduct and it will not be a workers matter in its settlement. Whoever wins, the workers will lose, unless they revolt against the entire domination of military or governing cliques.

OFFICER: Tell it to the firing squad.

PERCY: I shall have nothing to do with it, and you can do as you damned well like.

SCENE 17

ARTHUR *and* PERCY *see one another across the stage.*

PERCY: Are you alright feller?

ARTHUR: Yeah. Yeah, I'm…

PERCY: It's good to see you.

ARTHUR: And you Percy … I'm sorry.

PERCY: What for?

ARTHUR: I couldn't cope in solitary. They told me you'd broke … gone to the work camps. Once I got there I found out you hadn't. I felt pretty sick, Percy.

PERCY: They told me you had.

ARTHUR: Did they? And what did you say?

PERCY: Not a lot. I just thought if Arthur's gone to the work camp they must have knocked him about bad … so I'll stay even stronger … I'll do it for me and him … take it for both of us … I knew you'd have done it for me.

ARTHUR: But … I didn't. I just wish I'd kept to it … like you did.

PERCY: Give over. You were the one that did it! After you ran rings round the Tribunal … they had to admit there were political grounds for objection. Arthur … you beat 'em mate.

ARTHUR: You're a good lad Percy. Best mate a feller could have.

PERCY: Our day will come Arthur. Folk *will* listen! Stands to reason! It all adds up feller.

Percy Ellis remained a Marxist and a trade unionist for the rest of his days.

Enter SIS.

SIS: Hello Arthur.

ARTHUR: Hello Sis. You look more lovely than ever.

SIS: You look half starved. Come on.

ARTHUR: Where?

SIS: Our house. I'm feeding you. Then we have work to do. The revolution Arthur, after this madness folk will see it now, I'm sure of it! Come on.

ARTHUR: But your old one?

SIS: What about him?

Enter ISAAC.

ISAAC: Arthur ... come in.

ARTHUR: Mr Timmins ... pleased to finally meet you.

ISAAC: It's Isaac.

ARTHUR: Isaac.

ISAAC: You were right. It should never have happened. And they should never have treat you lads like they did either. I'm proud of you.

ARTHUR: Thankyou Isaac ... Sis ... I'm blacked all over the district ... no one'll give me a job ... you don't want me.

SIS: Then I'll get a job. I'm really proud of you, Arthur.

ISAAC: You're no coward lad that's for sure. Sit down kid ... look like you're stopping.

Arthur Gadiner joined the Labour Party in 1918. Blacklisted by the textile industry, he was unemployed until 1926, when he became a full time employee of the Labour Party.

There were more than 20,000 conscientious objectors, Quakers,

54

Liberals and Non-conformists as well as Socialists. After Arthur's appearance before the Military Service Tribunal they were forced to accept that there were political grounds for exemption.

He and Sis Timmins married in 1922. He was a councillor for almost 40 years, and elected Mayor of Huddersfield in 1941. He died in 1971.

Ladies and Gentlemen we are the Clarion Socialist Dramatic Society and thankyou for watching our play this evening.

– END –

SOCIALIST HYMNS

Hymn 1

Nay, speak no ill! A kindly word
Can never leave a sting behind,
And, oh! To breathe each tale we've heard
Is far beneath a noble mind.
Full oft a better seed is sown
By choosing thus the kinder plan,
For if but little good be known,
Still let us speak the best we can.

Give me the heart that fain would hide –
Would fain another's fault efface;
How can it pleasure human pride
To prove humanity but base?
No: let us reach a higher mood,
A nobler estimate of man –
Be earnest in the search for good,
And speak of all the best we can.

Then speak no ill, but lenient be
To others failings, as your own;
If you're the first a fault to see,
Be not the first to make it known.
For life is but a passing day,
No lip may tell how brief its span,
Then, oh! The little time we stay,
Let's speak of all the best we can.

Hymn 52

These things shall be! A loftier race
Than e'er the world hath known shall rise
With flame of freedom in their souls,
And light of science in their eyes.

They shall be gentle, brave and strong,
To spill no drop of blood, but dare
All that may plant man's lordship firm
On earth and fire, and sea, and air.

Nation with nation, land with land,
Unarm'd shall live as comrades free;
In every heart and brain shall throb
The pulse of one fraternity.

New arts shall bloom of loftier mould,
And mightier music thrill the skies,
And every life shall be a song,
When all the earth is paradise.

These things – they are no dreams – shall be
For happier men when we are gone:
Those golden days for them shall dawn,
Transcending aught we gaze upon.

Hymn 59

Ye sons of freedom, wake to glory!

Hark! Hark! what myriads bid you rise!

Your children, wives, and grandsires hoary,

Behold their tears and hear their cries –

Behold their tears and hear their cries –

Shall hateful tyrants, mischief breeding,

With hireling hosts a ruffian band,

Affright and desolate the land,

While Peace and Liberty lie bleeding?

To arms! To arms! Ye brave!

The avenging sword unsheath!

March on! March on!

All hearts resolved

On liberty or death

See now the dangerous storm is rolling,

Which tyrant kings confederate raise;

The dogs of war let loose are howling,

And lo! our fields and cities blaze –

And lo! our fields and cities blaze –

Shall we basely view the ruin

While lawless force, with guilty stride,

Spreads desolation far and wide,

With crime and blood their hands imbruing?

To arms! To arms! Ye brave! Etc

With luxury and pride surrounded,
The vile insatiate despots dare –
Their thirst for pride and power unbounded –
To mete and vend the light and air –
To mete and vend the light and air –
Like beasts of burden they would load us;
Like gods would bid their slaves adore –
But man is man, and who is more?
Then shall they longer lash and goad us?

To arms! To arms! Ye brave! Etc

O liberty! Can man resign thee,
Once having felt thy generous flame?
Can dungeons, bolts, or bars confine thee,
Or whips thy noble spirit tame?
Or whips thy noble spirit tame?
Too long the world has wept, bewailing
That's falsehoods dagger tyrants wield,
But freedom is our sword and shield,
And all their arts are unavailing.

To arms! To arms! Ye brave! Etc

Hymn 60

All are architects of fate
Working in these walls of time;
Some with missive deed and great,
Some with ornaments of rhyme.
Nothing useless is or low,
Each thing in its place is best;
And what seems but idle show
Strengthens and supports the rest.

For the structure that we raise
Time is with materials filled;
Our todays and yesterdays
Are the blocks with which we build.
Build today, then, strong and sure,
With a firm and ample base;
And ascending and secure
Shall tomorrow find it's place.

Hymn 64

Above the search for showy gold,
Its pomp, its pride, its power,
We place the glow of ruddy health –
Fair nature's kindliest dower,
We glory in the friendly sun,
The gentle, quickening rain,
The stars that kindle one by one
The moon that draws the main.

A simple walk of life is ours,
A heart from envy;
We pluck the humble wayside flowers,
And let the others be.

Not ours the feverish haste to reap
Where other men have sown,
The schemer's fears that murder sleep,
The heavy heart of stone.
Our homely wants – our food, our dress –
With ease are satisfied;
'Tis ours the cup of happiness
To eager souls denied.

A simple walk of life is ours, etc

The flowing gown, the lordy hall,

Men's empty words of praise:

These fretful pleasures quickly pall,

And tarnish golden days.

But walks across the scented mead,

By bank and prattling stream,

Ennobling thought and gentle deed,

Make life a blissful theme.

A simple walk of life is ours, etc

Hymn 67

I love a lonely hour at eve,
Or in the silent night,
When o'er the soul in stillness steals
A solemn, sweet delight,
To sit and think of things long gone
All blent with smiles and tears, –
The happy scenes and sunny loves
Of long departed years.

I love the look of gratitude,
The tear of pity's eye,
The word of hope, the laugh of love,
The sympathetic sigh;
And that dear woman's loving look,
Whose soul with virtue glows,
And deeply, keenly feels for all
Her suff'ring sister's woes.

I love the man whose soul disdains
To treat his kind with scorn,
However wretched be their lot,
However lowly born,
Whose chiefest end's to speak the truth,
To aid the world along,
And from the temples of all woe,
To cast out every wrong.

I love the land to labour on,

Although there's none for me;

And dear as light, and life, and love,

The nation that is free.

And, oh! I love, of all I love,

The dearest yet of all,

To see the poor man's rights restored,

And mighty tyrants fall.

Hymn 68

England arise, the long, long night is over,

Faint in the east behold the dawn appear;

Out of your evil dream of toil and sorrow

Arise, O England, for the day is here!

From your fields and hills,

Hark! The answer swells –

Arise, O England, for the day is here!

People of England! all your valleys call you,

High in the rising sun the lark sings clear:

Will you dream on, let shameful slumber thrall you?

Will you disown your native land so dear?

Shall it die unheard –

That sweet pleading word?

Arise, O England, for the day is here!

Over your face a web of lies is woven;

Laws that are falsehoods pin you to the ground;

Labour is mocked, its just reward is stolen;

On its bent back sits idleness encrowned.

How long while you sleep

Your harvest shall it reap?

Arise, O England, for the day is here!

Forth, then, ye heroes, patriots, and lovers!

Comrades of danger, poverty and scorn!

Mighty in faith of freedom, your great mother.

Giants refreshed in Joy's new-rising morn.

Come and swell the song,

Silent now so long;

England is risen! – and the day is here!

Hymn 81

Ho, thou traveller on life's highway,
Moving carelessly along,
Pausing not to watch the shadows
Lowering o'er the mighty throng:
Stand aside and make how feebly
Some are struggling in the fight,
Turning on thee wistful glances,
Begging thee to hold the light,

Hold the light!
Hold the light!
Brother, come and hold the light!

Look upon thy right; a brother
Wanders blindly from the way;
And upon thy left a sister,
Frail and erring, turns astray;
One kind word perchance may save them,
Guide their wayward steps aright;
Canst thou then withhold thy counsel?
No, but fly and hold the light!

Hold the light! etc

Hark! a feeble wail of sorrow
Bursts from the advancing throng,

And a little child is groping
Through the darkness deep and long;
'Tis a timid orphan shivering
'Neath misfortune's withering blight;
Friends, home, love are all denied her,
Oh, in pity, hold the light!

Hold the light! etc

Here, e'en here, in life's broad highway,
Are benighted wanderers found;
And if all the strong would heed them,
Lights would glimmer all around,
Acts of love and deeds of kindness
Then would make earth's pathway bright
And there'd be no need of calling-
Brother, come and hold the light!

Hold the light! etc